SO-AID-536

The Quite

Remarkable

Adventures of

the

Owl

and the

Pussycat

by

Eric Idle

Based on

the Poems,

Drawings,

and Writings of

Edward Lear

Additional

Illustrations by

Wesla Weller

Acknowledgments

This book would not have been possible without the collaboration, support, and encouragement of my friend and partner John Du Prez, whose wonderful companionship and brilliant musicianship inspired me and coaxed me forward when all seemed lost. His support and advice were inestimable, and my thanks are long overdue to him. I am indebted to Brenda Pope-Ostrow for her tireless editing, to Wesla Weller for her delightful art, and to Tom Hoberman, Sarah Winer, Mary Aarons, and Deborah Raffin for their unstinting encouragement. To my son Carey, my daughter Lily, and my beloved wife Tania, and finally to Edward Lear, whose love of children and nonsense has inspired this story.

E.I. 1996

Illustrations on pp. 3, 7, 8, 9, 10, 11, 13, 32, 73, 85, 86, 88, and 97 by Edward Lear.
Illustrations on the cover and pp. i, iii, 1, 4, 5, 6, 14, 15, 21, 27, 31, 33, 35, 37, 40, 42, 44, 47, 48, 54, 56, 58, 61, 63, 65, 68, 71, 72, 76–77, 79, 81, 84, 93, 99, 100, 102, 104, 106, 108, 109, 111, 117, 118, 119, 122, 123, and 124 by Wesla Weller.

ISBN: 0-7871-1042-6

Printed in the United States of America

A Dove Kids Book
A Division of Dove Entertainment, Inc.
8955 Beverly Boulevard
Los Angeles, CA 90048

Distributed by Penguin USA

Designed by David Skolkin

First Printing: October 1996

10 9 8 7 6 5 4 3 2 1

For Lily

Chapter One

There was once a young owl who lived by the shores of the great Lake Pipple-popple on the outskirts of the City of Tosh. He was a shy owl who preferred reading instead of flying about like all the other birds.

His friends were worried. "It's not natural," they said. "Owls is birds, and birds must fly. Fur rules the earth and feathers the sky."

But Owl would only sigh and turn his big round eyes back to the pages of his book, or he would pick up his guitar and play gently to himself for hours. He wasn't interested in flying or owling around. He was interested in the planets and the stars and the galaxy that he was a tiny part of, which was growing, just like him, a little bigger every day.

Whenever he grew tired of reading, he would pop across Lake Pipple-popple to visit the Principal Museum of the City of

Tosh. Inside the main hall there was a skeleton of an enormous dinosaur that he loved to gaze at, imagining what it must have been like when it was alive.

Now, the main activity of the citizens of Tosh was shopping, for which they were famous throughout the world, and almost everybody had heard of their famous shopping song, which went something like this:

The Shopping Song

Shopping, we're always happy when we're shopping!
We're always happy when we shop until we drop
In search of bargains we will never stop, stop, stop,
We'll shop and shop and shop, shop, shop!
(Repeat 130 times)

Chapter Two

One sunny afternoon Owl arrived in the City of Tosh on the very day of the Annual Festival of Shopping. The streets were crowded with shoppers, and there was a big parade led by the marching band of the Volunteer Fire Brigade. Everywhere there were balloon vendors, and ice-cream sellers, and umbrella stalls, and people shopping for souvenirs of shopping.

What immediately caught Owl's eye was the cats' chorus of majorettes marching behind the band: forty-six fabulous felines all in step, twirling batons and occasionally throwing them high into the air and catching them again. They were dressed in fluffy little pink outfits, and Owl was thinking they were the cutest things he'd ever seen when—*ouch!*—a baton landed on his head.

A CITIZEN OF TOSH SHOPPING

He found himself sitting on the pavement, gazing up into the eyes of a very concerned and very beautiful cat, who blushed wonderfully and said in a pretty voice, "Oh, gosh, I'm so sorry, the baton slipped. Oh, dear, are you terribly hurt?"

She was so lovely and Owl was so shy, he couldn't say a word.

3

The cat, thinking he was much more hurt than he was, began once more to apologize. "I'm *soooo* sorry," she said. "Heavens, I'm clumsy. You see, oh, golly, I'm not very good at this."

Owl could only stare at her. He had fallen in love at first sight.

"Can't you speak?" she said. Owl shook his head.

"Oh, dear," she said. "Perhaps ice cream will help."

Soon they were sitting in a small café ordering frozen rainbow ice while the cat fussed over him and insisted on staying with him until he was better.

He was quite unused to such attention, and when he finally regained his voice, he could only talk nonsense, saying he was in the habit of having batons land on his head, practically every day, in fact, and he actually enjoyed it (which goes to show the nonsense you talk when you fall in love). The cat laughed, assumed he was still dazed, and told him her name was Kitty, although everybody called her Pussycat. By the end of the ice cream they were getting along famously and had indeed become great friends. They were both thrilled to discover they loved visiting the dinosaur in the Principal Museum.

"Well, what are we waiting for?" said Pussycat excitedly. "Let's go right now."

The marching band was fast disappearing up the street, and behind them twirled the pretty majorettes.

"But what about the Shopping Festival?" asked Owl.

"Oh, phooey," said Pussycat. "The museum is much more fun than shopping. Besides, you can meet my uncle, Professor Bosh. He works there, you know."

Chapter Two
and a half

Presently the Owl and the Pussycat were standing by the left-hand foot of the gigantic dinosaur, whose bones towered above them like a prehistoric xylophone.

"They used to have feathers, you know," said Owl, "like a bird."

"Nonsense," said Pussycat. "Everyone knows they had fur like a cat."

It was their first argument, but friends can quite happily disagree on all sorts of important things, like whether or not dinosaurs had fur or feathers, and it didn't seem to matter at all. Owl had never felt happier in his life as they stared up at the huge creature. They hardly heard the footsteps behind them, and it was only after he hemmed and coughed that Kitty turned and recognized an elderly man with a long beard.

"This is my uncle, Professor Bosh. He is Professor of Biology."

"Wow," said Owl, who loved the science of living things.

"Pleased to meet you," said the Professor. "Would you two like to see something really special?"

He led them along musty corridors and up marbled stairways to the top of the building, where he took out a rusty key and unlocked a creaky door.

"This is my private collection," he said.

The room seemed to run the entire length of the building and had a glass skylight and a vaulted ceiling. It was covered in papers and books and jottings and notes, and along one side there were several large display jars.

Professor Bosh winked and, carefully locking the door, beckoned to them. Each jar contained a different, fabulous specimen. So different and fabulous were they that they have their own chapter.

Chapter Three

THE FABULOUS
PLANTS OF BONG

Owl could hardly believe his eyes. The jars were filled with the most amazing living things. The first contained a singing fish, which hopped from foot to foot and recited a song about codfish in a loud whale.

Cod, cod, cod!
That's the fish we adore.
We don't like herring,
We don't like plaice,
Offer us lobster, we'll laugh in your face.
What we want is cod!
It's the best fish, by God!
So give us a plateful
And we'll be quite grateful
For cod, cod, cod!

The second jar held the most extraordinary plant formed entirely of little pigs, which the Professor called by its common name, the *Piggy-wiggia.*

Next to it was a flower in the shape of a very comfortable armchair that Pussycat longed to sit on but was warned that perhaps she shouldn't, as it was in fact a flower and not a seat.

PIGGIAWIGGIA PYRAMIDALIS

ARMCHAIRIA COMFORTABILIS
(OR COMFY CHAIR FLOWER)

8

Then came a whole sequence of extremely odd flowers: parrot plants, nursery plants, crab trees, and chick plants.

Perhaps the most spectacular of these plants was the *Manypeeplia Upsidownia*, which consisted of a great many people hanging around all talking a great deal of nonsense.

"It's just like the government," said Professor Bosh.

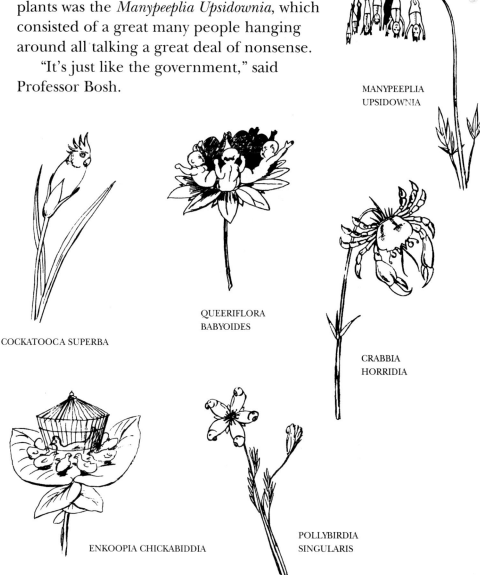

MANYPEEPLIA
UPSIDOWNIA

QUEERIFLORA
BABYOIDES

COCKATOOCA SUPERBA

CRABBIA
HORRIDIA

ENKOOPIA CHICKABIDDIA

POLLYBIRDIA
SINGULARIS

In the very next jar an elegant
ostrich observed them and became
very possessive of its boots. Pussycat peered
at them enviously.

The Professor winked and hurried
them along to a loudly buzzing jar that
consisted of hundreds of houseflies
flapping their wings and making a very
loud noise.

OSTRICHIA BOOTIDILIS

BLUEBOTTLIA BUZZTILENTIA

Beside the flies was a pleasant blue snake with a hat on,
who bade them "Good morning" in a polite voice,
while an umbrella beetle with a green parasol
crawled around his jar expecting
bad weather.

Owl and Pussycat stared at the jars
in fascination. They had never

seen anything like it in their lives.

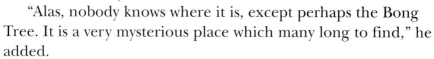

"Where did they come from?" asked Owl.

"They are all from the Land of Bong," said Professor Bosh.

"Where on earth is that?" asked Pussycat.

"Alas, nobody knows where it is, except perhaps the Bong Tree. It is a very mysterious place which many long to find," he added.

"What on earth's a Bong Tree?" said Owl.

"Aha," said the Professor, a gleam in his eye. "The Bong Tree is the very prize of the collection. Follow me." He led them to a huge oak door at one end of the room with a simple sign carved on it:

BONG TREE
EXTREMELY PRIVATE

"The Bong Tree is the oldest tree in the world," explained Professor Bosh as he knocked on the door. "Legend has it that it was one of the original trees in the Garden of Eden. There was the Tree of Life, the Tree of Knowledge, and the Bong Tree, which is the Tree of Evolution. Everything descends from it. It flowers only once every twenty thousand years and is the rarest and most prized of plants, because apart from anything else, the Bong Tree can walk!"

"Good heavens!" said Pussycat.

"And it can talk."

"Wow," said Owl. "A walking, talking tree."

"It is the only truly migratory tree," added Professor Bosh. "There is a bush that goes to the South of France for the summer, but that's really more of a shrub."

He knocked again. There was no reply. Puzzled, he pushed open the door, and his face fell.

"Good grief!" he said. "It's gone!"

The Sinister
Chapter Four

"Where is the Bong Tree?" asked a sinister voice. "Tell us and we'll let you go." Deep in the volcano underneath Mount Pipple-popple three young apprentice sorcerers were grilling a defenseless flower.

It was a long way from its home in the flower beds of Bong, where it was known for its extreme cheerfulness and ability to whistle and sing through adversity. Now it was bravely refusing to talk.

"The Fire Lord has been asleep for thousands of years. He's going to be very angry when he wakes up," said Flame.

"You have no idea how powerful he is," said Brimstone. "He is one of the seven sons of Lucifer, and *he* was thrown out of heaven for causing trouble."

PHATTFACIA SUPERBIA

"Dat's right. But he only wants de Bong Tree," said Flicker. "You he don't need."

"Why does he need the Bong Tree?" asked the little flower.

"What does it matter to you? Just tell us where it is and we'll let you go," said Brimstone.

"Hurry up. He'll be here in a minute," said Flame, "and he's really terrifying."

"We ain't kiddin' wid ya," said Flicker nervously. "Dis guy is really heavy."

"You'll be sorry," said Flame.

"We warned you," said Brimstone. "Now you're in for it. Tremble ye mighty, for the Fire Lord awakes!" and they fell to the floor and covered their faces to escape the cruel glare of their Lord and Master.

In the fireplace a tiny ball of energy burst into flames that flickered into the form of the Fire Lord, the dreaded Alchemist who lurks in the hearths and fireplaces of the world.

"I am the Fire Lord, son of Lucifer, Lord of the Volcano!" he breathed in a sulfurous voice. Little flames licked out of his mouth and sparks flew off his hair, and the terrified flower shrank back from his amazing heat.

"And I am Pyron, the Fire Lord's friend," said a fire-breathing dragon who hovered in the background and hissed flame at the frightened flower.

"So this is the pathetic specimen from the Land of Bong."

"Yes, sir, it is pathetic, isn't it, sir?" said the sycophantic Brimstone.

"Has it talked?" asked the Fire Lord.

"Not as such, sir, no, sir," said Flame, cringing.

"Oh, dear. Oh dear oh dear oh dear," said the Fire Lord in the most sinister and awe-inspiring tones.

The flower quaked to its roots.

"I'll give you one more chance," said the Alchemist, "and then I'm going to burn you," he added nicely. "So. Where *is* the Bong Tree?"

"I . . . I really don't know what you're talking about," bluffed the brave little flower.

"You know, the *Bong* Tree. Show him the book, Brimstone. And then we'll burn him to bits."

A huge old leather-bound book was opened for the flower to peer at. It wasn't like any other book you have ever seen, for it had moving pictures in it. Two of them were of the Bong Tree. The flower stared fascinated at a picture of the Bong Tree walking along a beach and another of it bathing in the ocean.

"Dis tree can walk," said Flicker.

"It can talk," said Flame.

"It can even swim," added Brimstone.

"And go shopping," said Flame rather unnecessarily.

"Enough!" exploded the Fire Lord. "The Bong Tree will not escape me this time. It must flower very soon, and when it does, I'll be ready, and I shall become the most powerful— But I don't need to tell you that," chortled the unpleasant Alchemist.

"Ha ha ha," said the sycophantic sidekicks, and they burst into a frightening song, dancing round the book-lined cave of doom, while Pyron the dragon roasted their heels.

Revenge Is Sweet
(In F sharp)

The Bong Tree has the strangest powers,
Every twenty thousand years it flowers.
But this time I will show it how
To take its final bough!

Revenge is sweet, revenge is swell,
We're gonna chop that tree to bits and burn it well.

The Bong Tree is the primal tree,
We'll saw it down, just you see.
Its seeds will sew the future though
Its future will be brief.

Revenge is neat, revenge is nice,
I'm gonna make that Bong Tree sad
It met me twice.

Revenge is fun, revenge is good,
We'll lumber it and chop it up to make firewood!

"Now. Where is the BONG TREE?" asked the angry Alchemist, and Pyron cruelly breathed a huge jet of fire on the plant.

The little flower shrank back from the flames and, desperately playing for time, said, "Why, I believe it's in the Principal Museum of the City of Tosh."

"Are you sure?"

"Of course."

"You'd better not be lying to me!"

The little flower shook its head.

"All right, Flame, Flicker, and Brimstone, go and fetch me the Bong Tree and, Pyron, keep an eye on them," and having said that, the horrid Alchemist burst into flames and, rapidly becoming smoke, disappeared up the chimney.

"Ouch," said Flame. "I'm singed."

"I wish he wouldn't do dat," said Flicker.

"He's a hard man to like," said Brimstone.

Chapter Five

"If the Bong Tree has such amazing powers," said Pussycat, "why would it run away?"

"Because it is due to flower," said Professor Bosh. "It must return home if it is to be safe. See, it has left a note."

The message was written on a simple piece of paper, wrapped up in a five-pound note, inside which Pussycat found seven sparkling seeds.

I must go back to the Land of Bong
To the land where the Bong Tree grows.
The riddle of the dinosaurs
Will help you find those secret shores.
Take with you these seven seeds,
For they will help you with your needs,
Against your enemies, to defeat 'em,
But remember, never, ever eat 'em.

They stared at the seven seeds that Pussycat was holding. Each was a different color of the rainbow. They glowed and sparkled in the palm of her hand and tingled as if she were being tickled.

"Bong Tree seeds," said the Professor.

"What on earth is the riddle of the dinosaurs?" asked Owl.

But he didn't get any further because at that moment, with a loud crash, Flame, Flicker, and Brimstone fell through the skylight and landed on a big pile of papers, which began to blow all around the room.

"All right, where's dat Bong Tree?" said Flicker.

"You're too late. It's gone," said Professor Bosh.

"Oh, dear," said Brimstone, as above them the fluttering wings of Pyron the Dragon flew off to warn the Fire Lord of their failure.

"He's going to be furious," said Flicker.

"Well, sorry to bother you," said Brimstone.

"Wait a minute," said Flame. "What are *they*?"

"Oh, they're just Bong Tree seeds," said Owl.

"They're nothing at all," said Pussycat too late.

"That's right, I forgot, they're nothing at all," said Owl hurriedly.

"Give dem to me," said Flicker. "Maybe dese'll keep him quiet."

"Shan't," said Pussycat defiantly.

"You have no choice," said Brimstone. "We'll just take them anyway," and he reached out his hand towards the cat.

Just then there came a terrible rumbling that shook the museum.

"It's the volcano," said Professor Bosh.

"It's dat Fire Lord," said Flicker.

"Told you he'd be mad," said Brimstone.

The three assistants raced to the window in fear as the rumbling spread from the top of Mount Pipple-popple. In the streets the citizens stared in horror at the gray clouds belching from the volcano. In the middle of this smoke a frightening figure materialized.

"Citizens of Tosh," it proclaimed, "I am the Fire Lord, the Lord of the Volcano. I can be your friend who fuels your fires and heats your food and keeps you warm in winter, or I can be your deadliest enemy." At this he let fly a thunderbolt, which smashed into the thatch of a nearby cottage. At once it burst into flames to the horror of the poor people who lived there, who could only watch helplessly as their home was engulfed.

"Let that be a warning to you."

The terrified citizens threw themselves to the ground.

"What must we do?" they cried.

"Bring me the Bong Tree."

The citizens looked around in consternation.

"Find the Bong Tree and bring it to me, or the volcano will erupt and the entire town will be destroyed."

Upon which the dreadful coils of smoke began to disappear back inside the volcano, and the terrifying apparition of the ancient sorcerer faded from their view.

"Well, at least we can take him dem Bong Tree seeds," said Flicker nervously.

"Yes, hand them over, you—"

But the room was empty. Owl, Pussycat, and Professor Bosh had slipped away down the fire escape.

A Bit on the End of Chapter Five

They were hiding in a tiny office off the main hall. The shadow of the dinosaur fell across the frosted glass. It seemed almost alive. The Professor was speaking urgently to them. "We must help the Bong Tree at all costs. It must flower safely. You two will have to go to Bong and warn it."

"However shall we do that?" asked Owl. "Nobody knows where it is."

"Remember the Bong Tree's message," said the Professor. *"The riddle of the dinosaurs will help you find those secret shores."*

"But we don't know what the riddle is," said Pussycat.

"You have the seven seeds," said Professor Bosh. "They will help you, but remember—don't eat them. Here, put the seeds in this," and he handed them a honey jar, into which he slipped the seeds and screwed the lid on tight. He gave them plenty of money, which they wrapped up in the five-pound note. "Now go," he said.

"Why aren't you coming with us?" said Owl, who was not very brave.

"I have to stay and look after my specimens," said Professor Bosh. "I'll try and hold them off. Now quickly, this way," and he let them out of a tiny back door into the street.

"Hurry to Lake Pipple-popple, take a boat, and follow the river to the sea. Good luck, and may God go with you." So saying, he ran off to the main hall shouting and yelling. The three burly assistants could hardly avoid spotting him, and they chased him round and round the dinosaur for about ten minutes before they finally cornered him.

"Gotcha!" said Flame.

"Give us dem Bong Tree seeds," said Flicker.

"You're too late," said Professor Bosh. "They've gone."

"After that cat!" yelled Brimstone.

"They won't get far," said Flame. "She stands out a mile in that costume."

Flame, Flicker, and Brimstone ran into the street in hot pursuit and stopped in amazement. In front of them the streets were full of pussycats in little pink majorette costumes all going home.

"I don't believe it," said Brimstone.

Chapter Six

We're on our way to sea
To see what we can see,
A fiddledee-dum, a fiddledee-dee,
We're on our way to sea.

Owl and Pussycat were singing their way along the lane that led to the lake to keep up their spirits. Behind them the sunset cast a glow over the silent city, tinting the smoldering skyline of Mount Pipple-popple with its rosy rays.

They gazed forlornly at the shoreline of the great Lake Pipple-popple. All the fishing boats had gone. There wasn't so much as an old tub left. They were stranded on the shore.

"Oh, no," said Owl.

"They must have fled when the volcano rumbled," said Pussycat.

"How on earth will we find the land where the Bong Tree grows if we can't even get across the lake?"

"Owl," said Pussycat. "Do you think you could fly me over the water?"

"Um, probably not," said Owl.

"Am I too heavy?"

"That sort of thing," said Owl evasively.

"Suppose you were to fly about a little and scout out what's ahead."

"What, and leave you behind all by yourself?" said Owl. "Never."

"Owl," said Pussycat thoughtfully after a little while, "you can fly, can't you?"

"Um, not as such, no," said Owl shamefacedly. "But I can play the guitar."

"Yes, I'm sure that's much more useful," said Pussycat, kindly hiding her disappointment. "Never mind. We shall just have to use one of the seeds." She shook out the seven seeds from the honey jar and gazed at them thoughtfully. Each was a different color of the rainbow.

"What do we do with them, I wonder?" she said.

"We mustn't eat them, whatever we do," said Owl.

"Of course, what we *really* need is a boat."

"Sure," said Owl, taking the green seed from her. It looked just like a pea. "I wish we had a boat, too, but all we've got is a stupid pea," and he tossed it into the water.

No sooner had the seed hit the water than the lake began to boil and bubble and something magical began to grow before their eyes. Something was sprouting on the sea. It wasn't a plant exactly; it was more of a sea-going vegetable. But what *was* it?

They watched in disbelief as tiny tendrils shot out and curled across the water, leaves lifted into spars, petals piled up into planks, stalks stiffened into stanchions, stems extended into sterns and descended into decks, while spiderwebs of rigging ran riot, and ropes curled crazily out of the swelling seed. Peas popped open into plump and comfy cushions, and a massive mast sprouted up into the sky from whose topmost spar a fabulous sail unfurled. They were looking at the most beautiful pea-green boat.

"Wow," said Owl. "It's a boat."

"Of course," said Pussycat. "They're *wish* seeds. You said, 'I wish we had a boat,' and now we have."

"Great. That means we've got six wishes left, so if we're feeling hungry, for example, we can just wish for strawberries and lobster and chocolates—"

"Oh, no," said Pussycat firmly, "we mustn't waste any. They're for emergencies only," and saying that, she stepped onto the pea-green boat and helped Owl aboard.

The bright ropes cast themselves off and curled up comfortably on the deck in little coils, the sail filled, and soon they were at sea. Behind them the sky was all a-fire with the sunset as they watched the smoldering volcano and the skyline of the City of Tosh disappearing below the horizon. Their adventure had begun.

Chapter Seven

(A Very Short Chapter)

"An owl and a pussycat!"

"D-d-d-dat's right," said Flicker, trembling.

"And who is this?"

The terrified assistants threw Professor Bosh to the floor in front of the Fire Lord.

"He was hiding de Bong Tree. He helped dem escape."

"Punish him!" said Flame.

"Yes, he should be punished if anybody should," agreed the sycophantic Brimstone.

"Oh, indeed I shall punish him by all means if he doesn't cooperate," said the Fire Lord. "But perhaps the Professor can tell me a little about the seven seeds."

"I won't tell you anything," said the old man.

The hot breath of the dragon scorched the Professor's bow tie. "Bong Tree seeds. Rainbow colored. Dubious value," said the Professor through tight lips.

"I don't believe you," said the Fire Lord. "Pyron . . ." The dragon blew fire at him again, and Professor Bosh dropped to his knees.

"All right," said the Professor reluctantly, "you win. You are too powerful for me. The seeds will help you if you wish to find the Bong Tree."

"Oh, but I do," said the Fire Lord. "Believe me, I really do. So what must I do with these seeds when I find them?" he asked his prisoner. The Professor refused to speak. The Fire Lord nodded, and the dragon once more breathed his hot breath all over him.

"You must eat them," said Professor Bosh.

Chapter Eight

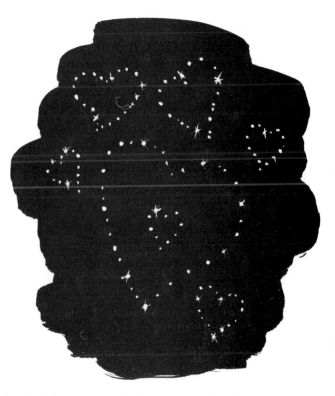

The Owl looked up to the stars above and said, "What an enchanting evening. How perfectly delightful this is." A light wind ruffled his feathers, and he looked across at the divine cat lying back amongst the plump pea-green cushions. She was gazing up at the bright stars waltzing above their heads. They seemed to her to form into hundreds of heart shapes.

Owl had pulled out the red seed and was gazing at it thoughtfully.

"Oh, Pussycat," he said finally. "It is such a beautiful night. How I wish I had a guitar so I could serenade you."

"Oh, no," said Pussycat. "You made a wish."

"Oh, dear," said Owl. "I didn't mean to." But it was too late. The tiny red seed was growing rapidly and turning into a beautiful guitar flower.

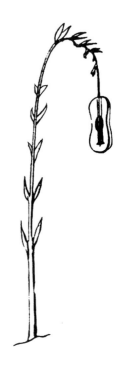

"Now you've wasted one of the seven seeds," said Pussycat. "We have only five left to get us all the way to Bong."

"Well, maybe it'll be useful," said Owl vaguely.

"What possible use is a guitar?"

"Sorry," said Owl. "I wi—" Pussycat clamped her paw over the Owl's mouth before he could say a word that rhymes with *fish*.

"Whatever you do, don't make another wish," she warned him.

"I—I was only going to say *if only* we knew which way to go."

"Oh, that's easy," said the guitar.

Owl was astonished. The small guitar plant was addressing them.

"You talk?" said Pussycat.

"Well, I sing," sang the guitar, and it played a short burst of flamenco. Pussycat applauded enthusiastically. Owl was a little jealous.

"How can you possibly know the right way to go?" he asked.

"Because I am from Bong," sang the guitar and pointed its long fretted neck towards a particular point on the horizon.

"Over there is the way to go," it sang, and as Owl adjusted course the small guitar began to play the most delightful waltz.

Moved by the music, Pussycat smiled at the Owl.

"Oh, Pussycat," said Owl, "I cannot say what is in my heart."

"Then sing it," said Pussycat.

"Oh, right," said Owl, picking up the small guitar. From somewhere inside himself he found the words

Oh, lovely Pussy, oh, Pussy, my love,
What a beautiful Pussy you are.

Pussycat smiled at him, and shy as he was, Owl was moved to sing from the very depths of his heart this impromptu serenade.

Owl's Serenade

Stars were in your eyes, my dear, the night we fell in love,
Stars were shining bright, my dear, the night we fell in love,
The pale moon shone so splendidly in heaven up above.
Stars were in your eyes, my dear,
This night was made for love.
Stars fell from the skies, my dear,
The night we fell in love.

Pussycat lay back on the pillows and gazed at Owl and thought she had never been so happy.

"Oh, Owl," she said, "you elegant fowl, how perfectly lovely you sing."

Above their heads the stars formed into dots of music while the beautiful pea-green boat headed off towards the land where the Bong Tree grows.

Chapter Nine

Dawn was breaking in the eastern sky, and on the deck
the Owl and Pussycat were gently dreaming. The little boat
held firmly to its course while the guitar snored away at the
helm. The sudden cry of a seagull woke it, whereupon it
yawned and stretched and stared at the horizon. After a
moment it frowned. Something it saw there disturbed it, so the
small guitar went over and shook Owl.

"What's up?" said Owl.

"There seems to be a ship," sang the guitar in a minor key.

"What's so bad about that?" said Owl.

"It's following us."

"And what's so bad about that?" asked Owl nervously.

"Well, it's not just a ship, it's a Pirate
ship!" sang the guitar, and in its fear it
began to play some anxious music full of
ponderous arpeggios.

Owl shinned up the rigging to get a
better look. There, sure enough, fluttering
from the mast of a Chinese junk headed
directly towards them, was a Pirate flag.

"It's not a Pirate flag," said Pussycat,

after Owl had woken her. "It *looks* like a Pirate flag, but on closer inspection it isn't a skull and crossbones at all. It's a large pie, with crossed knives and forks underneath."

"What?" said Owl.

"They must be Pie-rats," said Pussycat.

Sure enough, capering on the deck of the fast-approaching vessel was a crew of sleek ocean-going Pie-rats, singing in a slightly menacing key a Pie-rat song.

The Pie-rat Song

When I was a boy, I put to sea,
Yo-ho diddle-diddle dum-dum-dee.
It never did no harm to me,
Yo-ho diddle-diddle dum-dum-dee.
I didn't go to school or wear a hat,
Yo-ho diddle-diddle dum-dum-dee.
No, I became a Pie-rat.

Oh, we are Pie-rats, we like pie!
As Pie-rats we must eat or die.
Pie in your belly and pie in the sky,
Yo-ho-ho we're Pie-rats.

As the junk came alongside, two very athletic rats in Chinese kung-fu costumes leapt aboard.

"Who are you?" asked Pussycat politely.

"I am Yin," said the female rat.

"And I am Yang," said the male. "We are Pie-rats."

"What do you want?"

"Well, pie, obviously."

"We don't have any pie," said Pussycat firmly.

From the nearby deck the hungry Pie-rats began to sing again:

Custard pie, or strawberry pie,
Blueberry pie, or apple pie,
Give us pie, or you will die,
Yo-ho-ho we're Pie-rats.

"You're not really going to kill us, are you?" said Kitty.

"Probably not," said Yin.

"There's not much point if you don't have any pie," said Yang, and they began a frenetic display of kung-fu moves all round the deck. Owl rather thought they were showing off.

"We are the most ferocious Pie-rats on the seven seeds."

"Seas."

"You said 'seven seeds,'" said Pussycat suspiciously.

"Oh, did we? Um, must have been a slip."

"Wait a minute," said Owl. "I heard that."

"No, no, no. Just a slip of the tongue," said Yin.

"Do you have any seeds?" asked Yang innocently.

"Um, of course not," said Pussycat, looking firmly at Owl. She could see he was just about to say yes. Yang was looking at them suspiciously when at that moment a tiny rat from the top of the mast yelled, "Ship ahoy!"

All eyes turned to face another vessel that was fast approaching.

"Who dares approach us?" asked Yang. "*We're* the Pie-rats."

"It seems to be smoking," observed Yin.

It was true. There was a hazy sulfurous cloud hanging round the ship.

"Perhaps it has hot pies," said Yang optimistically.

The Pie-rats raced to the side of the ship and eyed it hungrily.

"What on earth is it?" asked Yin.

"Don't like the look of it," said Yang.

They watched the sinister vessel approaching. From the pea-green boat they could not see Flame, Flicker, and Brimstone climbing into a tiny rowboat on the other side of the ship. How could they have known that a fire ship was approaching them, packed to the gunnels with oil and tar and sacking and gunpowder, indeed anything that could explode and burst into flames? All the henchmen had to do was set fire to it and let it loose downwind, and it would engulf anything that lay in its path, such as a Pirate junk and a beautiful pea-green boat.

"Right," said Flame. "We lights the fuse, then in the panic and confusion, we nip aboard, grab the seeds, and scarper. Ready?"

"Ready," said Brimstone, striking a match and lighting a long fuse. They leapt into the little rowing boat and cast off.

"Look out!" yelled the lookout, way too late, as the fire ship burst into flames.

"Cast adrift!" yelled Yin, but nobody heard because in the panic several of the rats immediately jumped into the water.

"De first part of dis plan is woiking lovely," said Flicker.

"Just row," said Flame.

Hidden by smoke they rowed towards the pea-green boat.

Their fire ship rammed into the junk, and flames began to lick around the Pirate vessel. The pea-green boat was in great danger. At any moment the flames would spread and engulf them. Owl was desperately searching for a bucket when he ran flat into Yin and Yang, cool as you like, standing on the poop deck calmly whistling!

"What on earth are you doing?" said Owl. "Don't you know we're in deadly danger?"

"Yes," said Yin.

"So what are you doing?"

"Whistling," said Yang.

"This is no time for whistling," said the irate Owl.

"We're trying to whistle up a wind," said Yin.

"It'll blow us away from the fire ship," explained Yang.

"It's a good idea, Owly," said Pussycat. "Let's use a seed." She eyed the rats suspiciously. "Only don't let them see you."

Owl raced below and pulled out a blue seed. He carefully put the honey jar back on the shelf and, standing in the hatchway, said, "Oh, blue seed, be a wind. Oh, do become a wind. I *wish* you were a wind!"

No sooner were the words out of his mouth than the little blue seed rose in the air and floated around in tiny circles in front of his nose. Faster and faster it went, until finally it was going so fast, Owl couldn't see it anymore; he could only feel it, like a breath of air, then a breeze, and then a stiff strong wind that rattled the rigging and filled the sails of the beautiful pea-green boat. Within seconds the wind had pulled them clear of the fire ship.

"It's working," said Yin.

"See, the whistling worked," said Yang.

Pussycat winked at Owl. "Well done, Owly," she said.

In the stiffening breeze Brimstone was having trouble bringing their rowboat alongside. He reached up to try and grab the pea-green boat, but it was rocking hard in the swell. The wind continued increasing in violence so that everyone was hanging on for dear life, and as the pea-green boat was

light as a feather, it was suddenly lifted clear of the water and up into the sky, just as Brimstone made a grab for it. He found he'd grabbed at thin air, and with a cry he fell backwards into Flame and Flicker, knocking them over and capsizing their rowboat, so that they were all three thrown into the water.

"Oh, my gosh," said Owl. "We're flying!"

The pea-green boat was airborne.

"You idiot," spluttered Flame as they swam around desperately.

"Dis I don't believe," said Flicker as the beautiful pea-green boat sailed over their heads.

"*He* won't believe us," said Brimstone.

The wind whipped up a waterspout that soon put out the fire on the Pirate junk. Now that their ship was safe, the Pie-rats gave three hearty cheers for Owl and Pussycat, and everybody laughed and jeered at the three miserable apprentices as they swam off to face the wrath of the Fire Lord.

"Byee," shouted Yin and Yang over the side to their Pie-rat crew. "I guess we're going with them to save the Bong Tree."

"How did you know about the Bong Tree?" said Owl.

"Oh, uh, pure guesswork," said Yin.

"It's in the papers," said Yang vaguely.

Owl was not convinced at all, but he didn't have much choice in the matter, as the wind was lifting them and the beautiful pea-green boat high into the clouds.

Chapter Ten

The wind had dropped and the pea-green boat was floating along on the white fluffy clouds. It was really very pleasant sailing in the sky. The boat responded lightly to the tiller, its great big pea-green sail tugging them forwards, with the small guitar pointing the way. Pussycat was gazing over the side at the distant ocean miles below. Owl was dreaming at the tiller as Yin and Yang approached.

"So, what do the seeds look like?" asked Yang.

"What seeds?" said Owl.

"Bong Tree seeds," said Yin.

"Oh, nothing spectacular," said Owl.

"Then you *do* have some," said Yang. Owl had fallen for their little trap.

"Watch it, Owl!" yelled Pussycat. The rats had distracted him and they were heading straight for a large thundercloud. A flash of lightning and a deafening clap of thunder threatened to shake the little boat to pieces as they sailed into the sudden nighttime of the cloud's interior. Inside the storm the air was rushing around in all directions, and the sail began to creak and tug at the ropes, threatening to break away completely.

"We'd better get below
at once," said Owl. Just then
a giant flash of lightning
struck the mast, and the sail
collapsed on Pussycat,
knocking her overboard.

"Help me, Owl!" she
shrieked as she found
herself falling with nothing beneath her but the
big wide sea miles below.

Owl was tumbled upside
down by the lightning blast,
and when he had finished
bouncing, he looked around anxiously for
Pussycat. She was nowhere to be seen. He ran to the side of the
boat in horror and saw her falling helplessly. Without a
moment's hesitation he jumped straight over. He fell like a
stone, faster and faster until he found himself alongside
Pussycat. He stretched out and reached for her, caught her in
his arms, and instinctively swooped upwards.

"Oh, Owl," said Pussycat in admiration. "Look at you,
you're flying."

"Oh. Yes. So I am," said Owl. "Yippee! I'm flying! I can fly!"
and he did a little practice glide, turned a tiny somersault, and
flew her back up to the boat.

Yin and Yang grabbed them and hauled them in, and they
all hurried belowdecks, battening the hatches after them, for,
alas, they were still not safe. The boat itself was rapidly plum-
meting towards the pale earth, which rushed up to meet them
at a great rate. In the little cabin they anxiously awaited their

fate as the beautiful pea-green boat fell thousands of feet from the skies.

"Better hold tight," said Yang, and they grabbed cushions and held on to anything they could. Seconds later their boat hit the sea with a terrific splash and shot underwater to an enormous depth, where it landed with a bump on the ocean floor.

"Everybody okay?" asked Yang.

Pussycat pulled Owl from under the table where he'd slid. For the moment they were safe inside the cabin at the bottom of the sea with enough air to breathe, but how long would that last? A drip, drip, drip above their heads was turning into a steady trickle, which left pools of water on the floor of the boat. The boards above them groaned ominously, the leak was growing bigger by the minute, and the ceiling was threatening to burst under the pressure. Pretty soon they were ankle-deep in water.

"We're trapped," said Yang.

Pussycat had slipped over to the cupboard. She lifted the honey jar and unscrewed the lid. Reaching inside behind her back, she pulled out a seed. She nudged Owl, then holding the violet seed in her paw, she stretched expansively and said, "I wish we were out of here."

"We all wish we were out of here," said Yin, "but that's not going to help us very much."

"Well, it might," said Owl.

"Wishing doesn't just make things happen, you know," said Yang.

But to his immense surprise it did. The boat had suddenly started to rise.

"You see," said Pussycat triumphantly.

They rose swiftly now, like a cork underwater. Through the portholes they could see huge fishes looking in astonishment as they shot past them, and then at last they could see the sun. They had broken the surface. Gingerly they opened the hatches and stepped out onto the deck.

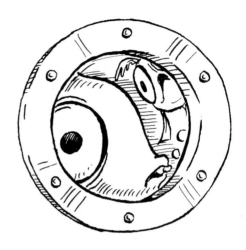

"We seem to be on some kind of reef," said Owl.

But it wasn't a reef, because to their surprise the boat continued to rise into the sky.

"We're still rising!" yelled Yin.

"How can that be?" said Owl.

"Oh, my gosh," said Pussycat. "I think we're on the back of a monster."

Chapter Eleven

"I thought they were supposed to help," said Owl as they continued to rise on the back of the unseen monster.

"What was supposed to help?" said Yang suspiciously.

"It's better than being trapped under the sea," said Pussycat, "and we seem to be headed for the shore."

Sure enough they were. Whatever they were on was wading towards a pebble beach with the pea-green boat wedged on its back. As it waddled ashore the shadow of the creature fell on the white cliff.

It was a dinosaur.

"It's just like our one in the museum," said Pussycat excitedly. "See, it is a fossil. It has neither fur nor feathers."

"I hope it isn't hungry," said Yang.

"Oh, listen, dinosaur music," twanged the small guitar. In the distance they could hear ancient rhythms as the dinosaur carried them along the beach towards the strange sounds. Rounding a rock, they came across a band of fossilized dinosaurs playing music on their bones.

"Look," said the knowledgeable guitar, "the percussive rhythms of the Bongosaurus, the sweet tinkling of the

Pianosaur, the sawing sounds of the Tricellotops, and the plinking of the merry Xylophon. They're playing pre-Cambrian music."

The dinosaur lurched towards the fossil band muttering a little song to itself:

Stegosaurs and Megosaurs,
And Segisaurs and Allosaurs,
Tenontosaurs and Brontosaurs,
And raspberries in hot chocolate sauce.

"Oh, dear. Sounds like it *is* hungry," said Owl.

Their stately progress towards the music was stopped by a sudden shout from Yang.

"Oy! Monster. Where do you think you're going?"

"Shh," said Owl. "Don't tell it we're here."

The great head of the dinosaur reared up on the bones of its neck and swung round to face the shipwrecked quartet on its back.

"Where on earth do you think you're going?" repeated Yang in a highly sarcastic voice.

The baleful eyes of the dinosaur crossed in deep thought as it stared down at the occupants of the tiny boat. "I'm going to the dinosaur dinner dance," it said after some reflection.

"No, you're not," said Yin.

"I think I am," said the dinosaur after a slight hesitation. "It's once every twenty thousand years. I may be a bit late."

"What on earth are you doing?" said Owl.

"Keeping it confused," said Yang.

"Best thing with a big beast," said Yin, nodding.

"They're going to upset it," said Pussycat.

"You know nothing, do you?" said Yang to the dinosaur in the same loud voice.

"Yes, I do," replied the dinosaur defensively.

"I bet you don't even know the riddle of the dinosaurs."

"Oh, yes, I do," said the puzzled fossil.

"All right. What is it, then?" demanded Yin.

"How did they know about the riddle?" Owl said to Pussycat.

In a halting voice the dinosaur recited the ancient riddle.

Backwards through time
Till time stands still
And light is frozen cold,
Walk across the Land of Water
To the ring of gold.
Fur and feather hold together,
Will unite to change the weather.

"That's it?"

"Not much of a riddle, is it?" said Yin contemptuously.

"Depends if you know the answer," said the dinosaur.

"What *is* the answer?" asked Yang.

"You mean you don't know it?" said the dinosaur. "You tricked me. I'm going to have to eat you for that."

"You can't eat us," said Pussycat firmly, "because you have no stomach."

"I have teeth, don't I?" argued the dinosaur. "So I can chew."

"You won't eat us," said Owl, "because I am your relative."

Everyone turned in surprise.

"Don't be ridiculous," said the dinosaur, gazing down at the small sanguine bird.

"As a matter of fact, you are my ancestor, and I can prove it to you," said Owl, picking up the small guitar. He began to play a little waltz, and soon the fossilized dinosaurs joined in, and to their accompaniment Owl launched into a most persuasive song.

Owl's Dinosaur Song

Since that late revolutionary dearie
And his great evolutionary theory
Mr. Darwin made plain for mankind to see,
He relates to the ape and the chimpanzee.
When paleontologists find a score
Of old bones on some distant South China shore
And they turn out to be a great dinosaur,
I'm ecstatic, so let me explain why:

I like dinosaurs,
I like dinosaurs,
I like dinosaurs,
For dinosaurs never look back.

Think of the fabled Diplodocus,
They said, "How unstable and odd he was,"
But you know two-thirds of his body was
Submerged so the beastie could swim.
These legendary lumpy monstrosities
Moved at highly surprising velocities
And rarely committed atrocities,
So join in my dinosaur hymn.

I like dinosaurs,
I find Tyrannosaurs
Are hardly ever bores,
Dinosaurs really are great.

"What is your point?" said the impatient dinosaur.
"I'm getting to it," said Owl.

People go into hysterics
When they think of the Archaeopteryx.
He'd clamber his way up a tree and then
This beastie would simply fall down again!
But one day in the early Jurassic times,
After one of his long and his classic climbs,
He flapped his arms and, though it seems absurd,
He flew and grew into a bird.

I like dinosaurs
More than hot chocolate sauce,
So let's all dance on these sunny shores,
For dinosaurs really are great!

I like dinosaurs . . .

"All right, you've convinced me," said the dinosaur. "I'll help you."

"We're trying to find the Bong Tree," said Owl.

"I knew it," said Yin.

"Oh, that'll be halfway across the Great Gromboolian Plain by now," said the dinosaur. "It's due to flower any day. We'd better hurry if we are going to catch it."

Sitting in the beautiful pea-green boat on the back of the fossilized dinosaur, they began to cross the Great Gromboolian Plain to the distant sound of dinosaur music.

Chapter Twelve

Three soggy henchmen were cringing at the feet of the Fire Lord, small puddles forming around them.

"A little wet, are you?" inquired the Fire Lord. "Damp from your exertions?"

Fires were smoldering all round him. Torches in the wall lit up the terrified features of Flame, Flicker, and Brimstone.

"Do you smoke?" he asked the terrified trio. "Oh, well, we'll soon see," and he cruelly hung them up over the fireplace.

"Smoking is very bad for your health." He laughed maliciously as steam began to rise from their dripping wet clothes. Fireflies danced in the smoky atmosphere, and an evil smell of sulfur hung about the place.

"The Bong Tree is only vulnerable on the day it flowers, and that's any day now. What am I going to do for the next nineteen thousand nine hundred and ninety-nine years if I miss this one, eh?" he asked the trembling Flicker.

"Uh, d-d-d-d-beats me," stuttered Flicker.

"You won't miss it this time," said Flame.

"No, I won't. But no thanks to you. Because I have a plan!"

"Oh, that *is* a good idea," said Brimstone.

"Shut up! You see a tree, like all living things, must have water, therefore I shall hide the sun."

"Where will you put it?" asked Flicker.

"I shall hide the sun with smoke!" said the Fire Lord. "And then the world will freeze."

He cast his arms wide and sprinkled some balsamic vinegar mixed up with a few herbs on the hearth in front of him. He then began to sing to himself as he worked on the magic spell.

Revenge is sweet, revenge is nice,
I'm going to make that Bong Tree sad
It met me twice.

The Bong Tree has the strangest friends,
But I'll make sure they meet their ends.
I'll seek them far across the sea,
They'll wish they'd not met me!
Revenge is sweet, revenge is swell,
I'm gonna find that Owl and Pussycat as well.

He then blew the mixture into the fire, which flared up dramatically. In response a low rumbling noise was heard below their feet, and the earth began to shake.

"A volcanic eruption?" said Flicker.

"Exactly," said the Fire Lord. "It'll create a smoke screen that will obscure the sun. The Bong Tree cannot survive long without water. Smoke will fill the pleasant atmosphere and a dreadful winter will lie across the face of the land."

"Well, what about us?" asked Brimstone, for he couldn't survive without water either.

The Fire Lord chose not to understand him. "You have one

more chance to redeem yourselves. The Owl and Pussycat are by now halfway across the Great Gromboolian Plain. Lie in wait for them, ambush them, make sure they don't escape you again," and so saying, the Fire Lord turned on his heels and left.

Outside, Mount Pipple-popple had begun to belch smoke, and the terrified citizens of Tosh looked up to see a huge fireball shoot out of the volcano high into the sky, trailing behind it plumes of smoke and gas, which turned the sun orange, as though it were about to set—which, in a sense, it was.

Chapter Thirteen

Halfway across the Great Gromboolian Plain a weary group of travelers was clustered in the shade of the great bones of a dinosaur. The plain was hot and dry with nothing in sight for miles and miles. Yin and Yang were examining some marks in the dusty surface.

"Tree prints," said Yin. "Look! See the mark its roots have made on the earth."

"No doubt about it," said Yang, rising. "That's Bong Tree spoor."

"I'd recognize it anywhere," said Yin. "Bong Tree. The King of the Forest."

"Pretty fresh, too. We can't be more than a couple of hours behind," said Yang.

"C'mon," said the dinosaur. "All aboard."

They climbed into the boat that sat neatly on the spine of the dinosaur and once more lumbered off behind the trail of tree prints. Over their heads a flaming fireball screeched across the sky, trailing a plume of brilliant colors, and plunged into the earth just below the horizon.

"What on earth was that?" asked Pussycat.

"Looked like a comet," said Owl.

"Certainly was close," said Yin.

"Can you smell smoke?" said Pussycat, sniffing.

Wispy trails of the fumes from the smoking volcano were creeping high behind them. Before them lay a devastated region where the fireball had plunged into the earth, burning everything in its path. The sun was starting to disappear.

"That's funny," said the dinosaur, looking up. "The bagpipes are flying."

Above them formations of flying bagpipes droned mournfully overhead, flying south in tartan formation like geese, honking and wailing.

"Oh, dear," said the dinosaur. "It means it's time for another Ice Age. The bagpipes fly south in search of malt whiskey whenever the cold is due."

"But an Ice Age isn't due for another twenty thousand years," said Owl.

"Perhaps it has something to do with the riddle of the dinosaurs," said Pussycat.

Backwards through time
Till time stands still
And light is frozen cold,
Walk across the Land of Water
To the ring of gold.
Fur and feather hold together,
Will unite to change the weather.

"Well, the weather's certainly changing," said Owl.

The Extremely Short but Fairly Sinister Chapter Fourteen

"It's working," said the Fire Lord with glee from the top of Mount Pipple-popple as he watched the darkening sky and the effect of the sudden winter on the landscape.

"My curse on the world is the reversal of all nature: the whitening of the ground and the blackening of the sky; the torturing cold to feet and fingers; the black, doleful bare trees; the gray, woolly sky."

"What about the people?" asked Pyron. "What will happen to them when all the water freezes?"

"May they cease to know the difference between their toes and their fingers, and may both be turned into icicles. And then the Bong Tree will freeze fast before it flowers, and I'll be able to hunt it down."

"And then?" asked the terrified dragon.

"And then, at last, the future will be mine."

Chapter Fifteen

The weary travelers were almost off the plain after lolloping along on the dinosaur's back for what seemed like days. In front of them the trail that they had been following suddenly divided in two. One set of tree prints led off towards the mountains, while another continued along the plain. Yang was puzzled.

"See, here they go in different directions," he said.

"What shall we do?" asked Pussycat.

"Hmm. Looks like we'll have to split up. The Bong Tree is clever, but it can't go two ways at once," said Yang. "But since we don't know which is which, we've got to follow both, just in case."

"You head up into the foothills," said Yin, "and we'll track this spoor as fast as we can, and then come back and join you."

Owl and Pussycat waved farewell to Yin and Yang, and the weary dinosaur turned its great skeletonic head towards the hills that abruptly rose ahead of them out of the Great Gromboolian Plain.

"Be careful!" shouted Yang as the two parties separated.

"Do you think they can be trusted?" asked Pussycat, watching them disappear into the distance.

"Oh, probably," said Owl.

"They knew about the seeds, and they knew about the riddle of the dinosaurs," said Pussycat. "Wasn't that a bit suspicious?"

"Well, the seeds are safely hidden in the honey jar, so it doesn't really matter," said Owl. "Don't worry about it."

An hour later, as their dinosaur climbed into the hills, a swirling mist enveloped them. Owl and Pussycat couldn't see where they were going at all. They were sitting on the deck of the beautiful pea-green boat, which was propped precariously on the spine of the dinosaur. On either side fragrant banks of thyme were blooming.

"We're lost in the Mists of Thyme," said the dinosaur, cheerfully sniffing the air.

"That's not thyme," said Pussycat. "That's smoke, that's what that is."

Already the sun had disappeared, and they could hardly see ten yards ahead of them.

"Oops," said the dinosaur, sinking into some soft red sticky stuff. Owl and Pussycat had the distinct impression that they were floating.

"Excuse me," said Owl, "but where exactly are we?"

"This is the Pits," said the dinosaur.

"Oh, it's not so bad really," said Pussycat.

"No, no," said the dinosaur. "We're in the Jam Pits. The famous Mulberry Jam Pits, which guard the northern entrance to the Land of Bong. Or is it the southern? Dearie me, I'm getting so sleepy. It must be the Ice Age. I think I'll just lie down here and nod off for another twenty million years or so."

"Don't sleep," said Pussycat. "What about us?"

"Oh, how dreadfully inconvenient," said Owl as the skeletal beast rolled over on its side and, snoring gently, sank luxuriously into the warm jam waves. Luckily for them, they were already in a boat, which soon floated free of the sleeping giant and began to carry them slowly backwards down the current of the sticky jam river.

"Hey," said Owl, "we're floating backwards, and we're in the Mists of Thyme."

"Oh, my gosh," said Pussycat. "The riddle of the dinosaurs. We're going backwards through thyme!"

Chapter Sixteen

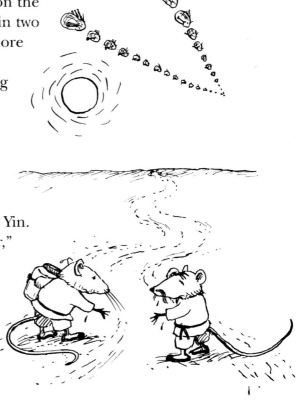

Somewhere on the Great Gromboolian Plain two Pie-rats were growing more and more alarmed. They had been following the tree prints for what seemed like hours and were very tired. Huge tartan flocks of bag-pipes flew constantly overhead.

"I don't like it," said Yin.

"I don't like it either," said Yang.

"You got any pie?"

"Not a slice," said Yang, "but I did grab some honey before I left the boat."

He pulled out Owl's honey jar. "Hey, there are some seeds in here."

"Stop!" said Yin as Yang was just about to pop one in his mouth. "Don't eat them. They're Bong Tree seeds."

"Oh, my," said Yang. "I didn't realize. Look how they sparkle. What are we supposed to do with them?"

"I don't know," said Yin, "but nasty things happen if you eat them."

The sky was darkening, the light was fading, and there was a distinct chill on the day.

"Don't you get the feeling that these tree prints are a little too regular?" asked Yang.

"Hmm. Almost as if someone had made them as a tra—"

But Yin never completed the sentence, for suddenly the earth caved in and they fell into a big pit.

Flame, Flicker, and Brimstone rushed forward excitedly.

"Is it them?" asked Flame.

"Nah. It's dem dam rats," said Flicker.

"Where are Owl and Pussycat?" asked Brimstone, but Yin and Yang, mortified at being caught, would not say a word.

"Never mind," said Flicker. "De Fire Lord will soon make dem talk."

Chapter Seventeen

The beautiful pea-green boat was floating gently backwards through thyme down the jam river. As Owl and Pussycat drifted slowly downstream (or downjam), they didn't see a tree watching them. It was an old tree of great dignity; a tree that moved slowly forwards once they'd passed, panting heavily, staring up anxiously into the clouds of smoke that obscured the sun.

"I think we're lost," said Pussycat, shivering in the sudden cold.

"Perhaps I'd better pop ashore and scout out the lay of the land."

"Oh, Owly," said Pussycat affectionately, "do be careful. I've grown very fond of you.

Indeed, if we ever find somewhere sensible again, I could quite happily—"

"What?" said Owl.

"You know. The M word," said Pussycat.

"Margarine?" asked Owl.

"Not margarine," said Pussycat. "Oh, do let us be married, too long we have tarried," she suddenly blurted out.

Owl went pink all over. "M-m-marry me?" he stuttered. "But what shall we do for a ring?"

"Oh. Yes. I don't know," said Pussycat at a loss.

Owl had a sudden inspiration. "We'll wish for one!"

"Do you think we should?" asked Pussycat. "The seeds are really for emergencies."

"This *is* an emergency," said Owl. "We *need* a ring. We'll use the yellow seed," and he raced belowdecks to the cupboard where he kept the honey jar.

The cupboard was bare.

"Oh, no," said Owl in despair. "The seeds are gone!"

"I'm afraid Yin and Yang have taken them," said Pussycat.

"Oh, no, oh, no," said Owl. "What shall we do for a ring?"

"What shall we do to find our way to Bong?" asked the practical cat, "for we are now quite lost and without a single wish seed!"

"I'll go and fly about and see what I can," said Owl.

"Are you sure you should?" said Pussycat. "We have never been parted since the moment we met, and now we are engaged, even though we haven't got a ring, and oh, dear, Owly, I should be most dreadfully upset if anything happened to you."

"Nothing's going to happen to me," said Owl with a little more confidence than he in fact felt. "I'll simply scout out the land and fly straight back."

He would have loved to kiss her, but it didn't seem quite right until he had the ring, and in any case he was desperately shy, so Owl shunted up the mast and flapped his wings as if he had done it all his life and fluttered off uncertainly towards the jam bank.

"I'm most dreadfully tired," said Pussycat. "All this emotion. I think I'll take a quick cat-nap while he's gone," and so saying, she lay down on the deck and promptly fell into a deep sleep.

Chapter Eighteen

Yin and Yang stood trembling in the firelight before the Fire Lord's hearth, captives in the cavern underneath Mount Pipple-popple. Flame, Flicker, and Brimstone smugly gloated over their capture.

The Fire Lord was struggling to understand the story they were telling him. He seemed less than pleased.

"Let me understand this," he said in his deep voice. "You made *false* Bong Tree prints?"

"That's right," said Flame. "Clever, eh?"

"You mean you found the *real* Bong Tree prints?"

"Dat's right. Den we made decoy ones and captured dese two Pie-rats," said Flicker. "Someting der madder?" he asked, dimly aware that the Fire Lord was not happy.

"You found the *real* Bong Tree prints and you didn't come back and tell me?!"

"Oh, yes. Oh, no. That is to say, oh, dear." They threw themselves on the ground.

"You idiots! Saddle my dragon," yelled the irate Fire Lord, and he stormed out of the room.

"You know he's quite mad," said Yin calmly to the cowering trio.

"Bonkers," added Yang. "I pity you."

"How do you think you are going to survive anyway?" said Yin. "You can't last without water either."

It was quite true. How *could* they survive without water? It was all right for him, he was a Fire Lord. Show him water and he would flare up so quickly, he'd have to explode to let off steam.

"This is an absolute disaster," said Flame. "We're all going to perish."

"Is that dragon ready yet?" said the Fire Lord, returning. "It's time to trap the Bong Tree." He seemed almost cheerful.

"Are you sure this is such a—" Brimstone faltered.

"Such a what?"

"Such a good idea."

The Fire Lord widened his eyes in the most terrifying manner.

"Actually, I think it's not a good idea. It's a *great* idea," Brimstone said quickly. "Fabulous. To freeze everything. How clever and amazing you are. You will rule over the whole world. Even though it'll all be dead."

"What?"

"Frozen. Not dead."

"After the ice comes the fire," said the Sorcerer as he leapt onto the back of Pyron and rode off into the sky.

"You won't survive that either," said Yin as they were being led down into the dungeons. They were thrown roughly into a damp cell.

From a pile of straw an old bearded figure rose to greet them.

"Professor Bosh, I presume," said Yin.

Chapter Nineteen

Owl hadn't gone very far when he flew slap into a frozen rainbow. His wings were icing slightly and he had been having difficulty flying when suddenly he found himself spread-owled against a slice of ice.

"What on earth is this?" asked Owl. It was about five yards round and formed entirely of rainbow-colored frozen light, and it arced off above him into the sky for what seemed like miles.

"It's a frozen rainbow, of course," said a most peculiar person. He had an extremely large head on a very short body. "You're not supposed to fly into them."

"Wow," said Owl. "I never saw one of those before."

"I never saw one of you before," said the strange man. "What an extra-ordinary creature you are, to be sure."

"You're a fine one to talk," said

Owl. However, he remembered just in time to be polite. "I'm an Owl."

"And I am the Yonghy-Bonghy-Bo," said the strange person proudly. "From the shores of Coromandel, fabled in rhyme and song. My card." And he handed Owl a rather crumpled ace of spades.

"Pleased to meet you," said the Owl.

"Of course you are," said the Bo. "Pink geraniums in sunlight."

"What?" said Owl.

The Bo gave him a huge wink. Owl was puzzled. "Can I climb the rainbow?" he asked, thinking he might find out where they were.

"You might. Then again you might not," said the Bo enigmatically. "It's just the tip of the Ice Age, you know. Here, have a piece," and he broke off a chunk of the rainbow-colored light and handed it to Owl.

"Uhm. I've never tasted light before. It has a peculiarly tingly taste."

"That's because it's trying to move very quickly, but it's frozen, so it can't. Each color is a different flavor," continued the Bo. "Red is red currant, orange is orange, green is lime, and so on."

"It tastes of tingles," said Owl.

"Even better when it's cooked," added the Bo.

Owl did not see how you could possibly cook frozen light. Surely it would melt and then you wouldn't have anything left to eat. At the very least the moment it ceased to be frozen it would start zooming off in all directions at the most fantastic speed before you even had a chance to take a bite.

"You've heard of a light snack, haven't you?" argued the Bo.

Owl conceded he had.

"And fast food? Well, there you are, then. Professor Bosh had a recipe for a light pie that was absolutely delicious," added the Bo.

"Professor Bosh? You know him?" asked Owl excitedly.

"Never heard of him," said the Bo.

"What nonsense you speak," said Owl.

"Why, thank you," said the Bo. "That's what we speak here, you know, *Nonsense*. It's the most wonderful language once you get to know it. You can express the exact opposite of anything you want, and of course, the lemon-yellow grass slithers down the old dirt road."

"What?" said Owl.

"Just a well-known phrase or partridge," the Bo added non-sensically.

Time was too short for all this nonsense. "Do you suppose you could help me look for the land where the Bong Tree grows?"

The Bo looked at him, turned round three times rather mysteriously, and replied in rhyme.

> *A strange little Owl asked the Bo*
> *Which was the right way to go.*
> *He said, "If I knew, I would go that way, too,"*
> *And he did, so he went, cheerio.*

And off he went, licking his limericks.

Above Owl's head the sky was darkening, which was surprising, since it wasn't even lunchtime yet, and it was hard to see any distance at all because of all the smoke. Owl's wing feathers were icing fast, so he decided it would be more sensible to climb the frozen rainbow and see what he could from the top.

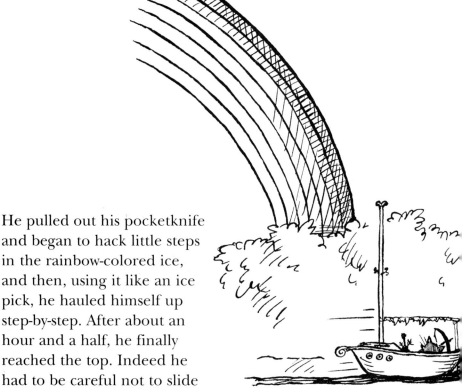

He pulled out his pocketknife
and began to hack little steps
in the rainbow-colored ice,
and then, using it like an ice
pick, he hauled himself up
step-by-step. After about an
hour and a half, he finally
reached the top. Indeed he
had to be careful not to slide
straight back down the other side,
because light is very slippery when frozen, but it
was all worth it for the wonderful view.

Behind him lay the Jam Pits, and the great jam river (where
the logjams are in winter), and he could clearly see Pussycat
asleep under a pea-green parasol on the deck of their boat. On
either side of the river huge forests lay, and just ahead there
was a frothing something that made a great roaring sound that
he couldn't quite make out. Beneath him, bordering the
forests, stretched a land made completely of water, like an
island in reverse.

"Of course," said Owl, "it's the Land of Water from the riddle of the dinosaurs. But you can't possibly walk across it."

By now the smoke from Mount Pipple-popple, combined with the deadly debris from the Fire Lord's comet, was drifting towards him and beginning to obscure the fine view that he had.

"I'd best get back to Pussycat before she wakes," said Owl, looking down to where their boat had been only a few seconds ago. But it had drifted farther off. He looked below him and sure enough he caught a glimpse of the pea-green boat through the swirling smoke. It was floating downstream, and horror of horrors, it was headed towards what he now realized were jamfalls (huge waterfalls of jam) that cascaded over a cliff, before plunging onto frothy rocks beneath.

Owl leapt to his feet in alarm and yelled, "Look out, Pussycat!" But he should have followed his own advice, for the top of a frozen rainbow is particularly slippery. In attempting to warn Pussycat of the tremendous danger, Owl completely lost his footing and began to slip and slide down the other side.

"Oh, dear, oh, dear," said Owl, gathering speed as he toboganed towards the ground, which seemed to be racing up to meet him at a fantastic rate. He was only grateful that it was apparently the Land of Water below.

Chapter Twenty

Owl had had no time to warn poor Pussycat. She lay fast asleep on the deck of the beautiful pea-green boat, floating slowly backwards towards the roaring jamfalls.

It was the small guitar which noticed the danger. It began playing dramatic chords and jumping up and down till Pussycat woke out of a beautiful dream in which she and Owl were being married by a turkey.

"Whatever is it?" asked Pussycat.

They could hear the most alarming roaring noise.

"It's falls!" said Pussycat.

"Quickly jump overboard," sang the guitar.

"I can't possibly," said poor Pussycat. "You see, I can't swim."

"Oh, dear me," the guitar sang fretfully. "Whatever are we to do?"

"Save yourself," said the brave cat, "for you are wood and can float."

"What, and leave you?" sang the guitar. "Never."

"Hurry, you must," said Pussycat, for they were now within ten yards of the brink of the jamfalls, and she could see how high they were. In seconds they would surely tumble over the brim and smash to pieces on the rocks beneath.

Pussycat gripped the small guitar and held it firmly as the tiny boat was drawn slowly but surely to the lip of the falls. She closed her eyes and prayed. "Good-bye, Owly," she said. "I loved you dearly."

She held her breath, expecting the sensation of falling. Nothing happened. After a moment she opened her eyes. They were stuck fast at the very top of the falls. The jam had frozen solid!

"Of course, the Ice Age," said Pussycat. "How fortuitous. How lucky that cats have nine lives. I think that was at least two of them." Gingerly she stepped out of the boat onto the frozen jam.

"It seems quite safe," she said to the guitar, "if a little slippery."

The guitar played a few grace notes, indicating it would much rather stay where it was, thank you, and settled in for a short recital. Reluctantly leaving the guitar, Pussycat slowly made her way to the bank and then set off into the forest to look for Owl.

Chapter Twenty-one

Owl, meanwhile, was sliding down the frozen rainbow at a fantastic pace like a toboggan out of control. Below him stalagmites and stalactites plopped and sploshed into the blue-green water, making fabulous music and forming fantastic shapes in the midst of which about a dozen water maidens were elegantly playing.

To their intense surprise Owl landed among them with a tremendous splash.

"Just dropped in," he said in a vain attempt to regain his dignity.

Beautiful caverns of aubergine colors and pools of liquid blue crystal-clear grottoes surrounded him. In the midst of this the surprised water maidens were leaping in every direction, shrieking and yelling. These totally see-through but perfectly formed young things, made entirely of water, were absolutely terrified by his sudden plunge down the rainbow into their world. Owl tried to calm them, but they were splashing around, yelling, and making a terrible commotion when suddenly the waters parted and the majestic figure of the Queen of the Water arose from the crystal depths. Owl thought that after Pussycat the Queen of the Water was the most beautiful creature he had ever seen.

"Girls, girls, please," she said, trying to calm her terrified minions. "Please welcome this soggy bird to our watery world." Rather reluctantly they performed a little wet water ballet, singing a damp greeting.

> *Welcome to the Land of Water,*
> *We are the Queen of the Water's daughters.*
> *We're always going with the flow,*
> *Because we're made of H_2O!*

The Queen rose to make a speech. "Dear visitor," she said, "honored, unexpected guest, my husband and I—"

Although it was very rude and a tremendous breach of protocol, Owl simply had to interrupt her. "Do you know the riddle of the dinosaurs?"

"No," said the Queen. "What is it?"

Owl closed his eyes and recited the riddle.

Backwards through time
Till time stands still
And light is frozen cold,
Walk across the Land of Water
To the ring of gold.
Fur and feather hold together,
Will unite to change the weather.

"That's pure nonsense," said the Queen.

"Yes, that's what they talk around here," said Owl. "We are searching for the Bong Tree to warn it of the Fire Lord, and we need your help."

"It doesn't live here," said the Queen of the Water.

"Well, we have been backwards through time, and I have just slid down the frozen light, but how can I walk across the Land of Water?"

"You can't," said the Queen, "unless it freezes."

"Of course, that's it," said Owl. "The Ice Age is coming."

"Oh, no!" screamed the water maidens. Ice ages are not particularly amusing when you are made of water.

"What is the ring of gold?" asked Owl.

"Oh, I know what that is," said the Queen. He struggled to hear what she was saying.

"It is vitally important that you shrimbumble . . ."

"What?" said Owl, for alas the Queen of the Water was rapidly freezing up and her voice was becoming slurred.

"You muushrhemb . . ."

Owl leaned closer. She had frozen solid. The water maidens, already blue with cold, were highly agitated.

"Do *you* know the answer to the riddle?" asked Owl urgently.

"It's something to do with the Bong Tree, but you must go

and find the ring, for we shall be ice quite shortly," said the nymphs, rapidly freezing up.

"Which way do I go?" asked Owl.

"Follow your nose," they said and then, "Sorry, we have to go, because we're turning into snow." Before his eyes the lovely water nymphs were seizing up and freezing up and becoming ice maidens—solid crystals of frozen female form.

"Oh, dear," said Owl. "They've all become ice."

Chapter Twenty-two

Pussycat was lost. She had been wandering in circles for hours inside the forest and was about to give up in despair when through the trees she saw the oddest procession. The walking fish was in the lead with a slight smile on its lips, and strapped to its back was the armchair plant. Snuggled comfortably in the armchair was the baby flower, the *Piggy-wiggia*, and the *Manypeeplia Upsidownia*. Behind them came the ostrich, who had the hatted snake riding on it, beside the parrot plant, the chick flower, and the crab tree, and bringing up the rear was the beetle with

the parasol in a buzz of buzzfly flowers.

"They're Professor Bosh's specimens," she realized. "They must have run away," and she ran forwards to greet them.

"What's happened? Where are you going?" she yelled, but they paid no attention to her. "Remember me, Professor Bosh's niece?" They said not a word in reply, looking neither to left nor right, but slowly trudging on deeper into the woods.

"Is he all right?" she asked, quite worried about her uncle, but the strange creatures simply ignored her and marched off into the Mists of Thyme.

Was she dreaming? Pussycat pinched herself hard. No, she definitely wasn't dreaming. Had they not seen her? Had she become invisible? It was very distressing. Tired, hungry, and lost, Pussycat sat down beneath a tree and despaired.

"Oh, Owly," she said, "where are you?"

Chapter Twenty-three

Owl was freezing. He was walking across the Land of Water, but how much farther could he walk? He gritted his frozen teeth and pulled his feathers in against the cold. Around him everything was white. The Fire Lord's curse to hide the sun from the land and freeze the water was rapidly taking effect.

Owl trudged painfully across the arctic landscape as the chill wind whipped in from the north. Ahead of him he spotted a night watchman wrapped in rags, huddled over a blazing brazier.

"Better hurry, pal," said the watchman, indicating a water clock, "or you may be too late."

"Too late for what?" asked Owl with difficulty, for he was now bitterly cold. He tried to reach out to the brazier for warmth, but even the fire was frozen solid. He looked at the water clock as it struck midnight, and then the final trickle froze and time itself stood still.

"Of course," said Owl, "frozen time so *time stands still*." The riddle was finally becoming clear to him. But, alas, too late, for the watchman had become an icicle and now Owl, too, began to freeze; first his feet and then his knees, until very soon he could not move at all, and his eyes started to glaze over, and he could only sigh and say, "Oh, Pussycat, where are you?" before his very breath froze solid. Poor Owl was totally frozen!

Chapter
Twenty-four

The Fire Lord was high in the sky on the back of his favorite dragon, halfway across the Great Gromboolian Plain. He was following the tracks of the Bong Tree, which he could see quite clearly below him. He could see the false trail left by his idiot henchmen, and the real Bong Tree prints leaving the plain and heading off into the foothills.

"Oh, bother," he said to Pyron, "it's gone into the forest."

The tracks showed where the Bong Tree had entered the woods, but there was no trail visible now, just miles and miles of virgin forest.

His eyes soon picked out the Jam Pits, and he followed the course of the great jam river. "Hello," he said to himself. "What's that?"

It was the beautiful pea-green boat, stuck fast on the brim of the jamfalls. He reined in his dragon and pointed its nose towards the boat.

"The Owl and the Pussycat went to sea in a beautiful pea-green boat," he said to himself. "Well, well, well, the Bong Tree cannot be far away."

It was indeed very close. At that very moment the Bong Tree was slowly walking down a frosty trail in the middle of the forest. All the tall trees bowed their heads in salutation as it passed. This was unfortunate for the Bong Tree, for they gave away its position. From the sky the Fire Lord could see the path the Bong Tree was taking through the woods.

"So there you are," he said as he watched the wave of trees bowing in respect, and he reined in the dragon and sent it plunging towards the earth.

Chapter
Twenty-five

Afterwards everyone agreed it was the Pig who had
saved them. Pussycat was desperately looking for Owl, but she
was completely lost in the mysterious woods when suddenly
right before her she saw a large Piggy-wig with a ring at the end
of his nose.

The Pig was pink and covered in little ginger
hairs, and she only noticed him because
he was doing a strange dance to warm
himself up.

"I'm so cold," sang the Pig. "I'm
cold, but I'm cool. Oh, boy, I'm so
cool. But I'm so cold, too. Oh, brother,
I'm cold."

Pussycat, being very well brought up,
didn't like to interrupt, since he was shak-
ing his large Piggy tushy and waddling
around in the most unusual way while he
sang a song that went something like
this . . .

The Pig's Song

Do the Piggy shuffle, do the Piggy strut,
Shimmy with your tushy, and shake your Piggy butt.
Do the Piggy reggae and rap the Piggy rap,
Dig the locomotive Pig and tap the Piggy tap.
Dance the Piggy ballet and really shake your wrist,
Do the Piggy cha-cha-cha and twist the Piggy twist.
Rock the Piggy rock 'n roll and really cut a rug,
Jig the Piggy-wiggy and frug the Piggy frug.
For I am Pig. Dig. Yes, I'm Pig.
I don't give a fig if you don't like Pig,
For I am me, that's what I am,
A porcine piece of dancin' ham.

and he looked up suddenly to see Pussycat watching him, spellbound.

"Don't you know it's quite rude to stare at people?" said the Pig.

"You are not people," said Pussycat.

"That's true," he conceded, "and very well observed. I suppose you're probably lost."

"Well, as a matter of fact, I am," said Pussycat nicely.

"Everyone is round here. Except for me. I can't get lost. People have been telling me to for years, but I can't. It's the ring, you know. It invariably leads me home by the nose."

She had indeed been eyeing the magnificent ring in his nose, wondering whether he might be tempted to part with it.

"Why ever would you want to get lost?" she asked politely.

"To get away from myself."

"But that's nonsense."

"Of course it is," replied the Pig.

"It makes no sense at all," said Pussycat, outraged.

"Oh, thank you. How very kind you are," said the Pig, highly complimented.

"Why on earth would you want to get away from yourself?" persisted Pussy.

"Oh, you don't know the piggy prejudice we porkers have to face. You have no idea what it's like to look someone in the face and know that all they can see is a bacon sandwich. You can't possibly tell what it is to lie in the sun with someone rubbing oil on you and know they're thinking only of grilled pork chops. You don't know the misery of having someone you love look at your backside and think, 'Hello, it's ham time.'"

"Well, we all have our problems," opined Pussycat. "I have lost my best friend."

"Congratulations," said the Pig.

"It's nothing to be proud about, you know."

"A friend in need is a friend in porridge," said Pig.

"But that's nonsense."

"Exactly. And first-rate nonsense, too."

"Why are you so proud of nonsense?"

"What's so great about sense? The rest of the world thinks it's sensible, and look how screwed up it is. So there, ha ha ha, yarty tarty tarty."

"I'm afraid I don't understand," said the puzzled cat.

"There you go, you see. Trying to make sense of everything. Your head isn't any use here. You must think with your heart."

"Why would you think with your heart when you have a perfectly good brain?"

"Dinosaurs had two brains, one in their backsides, and it didn't stop them from becoming extinct. So my motto is, 'Have plenty of strawberry jam and all will be fine.'"

"We left our dinosaur in the Jam Pits. It didn't seem to do her much good."

"The Jam Pits!" said Piggy, pricking up his ears. "You know where they are?"

"I might," said Pussycat, who could sense a deal, even if it was a nonsense deal.

"Oh, I adore jam. I can wallow in jam all day. It's Pig heaven."

"Well, it is only mulberry jam. . . ."

"Mulberry jam, oh, no, that's my favorite. Oh, please, please tell me where to find the Mulberry Jam Pits."

"I might," said Pussycat, prevaricating.

"Oh, I'll do anything for mulberry jam. If I help you find your lost friend, will you tell me where they are?"

"It's a deal," said Pussycat.

Chapter
Twenty-six

Deep inside Mount Pipple-popple, Yin, Yang, and Professor Bosh were sitting dismally in their dungeon. Beside them the little *Phattfacia* flower kept whistling cheerfully.

"We've got to do something. If the spell isn't broken soon, it'll be too late," said Professor Bosh.

"How do you break spells?" asked Yin.

"Let's see, well, reversing the curse, some kind of antidote, true love traditionally can do it, a kiss, a pure heart, there's lots of ways. We've simply *got* to get out of here."

"Will you please stop that cheerful whistling," said Yang. "It's beginning to get on my nerves."

"Why don't you use a seed?" suggested the *Phattfacia Superbia.*

"What did you say?" said the Professor.

"They've got three Bong Tree seeds in that jar, you know," said the flower.

"You have the Bong Tree seeds?" said the Professor, staring in disbelief at the honey jar Yang was holding.

"Well, yes," said Yang, unscrewing the lid. "We borrowed them from Owl accidentally."

"Why didn't you tell me?"

"Well, we didn't ask him," said Yin shamefacedly.

"That's not the point," said the Professor excitedly. "They're *wish* seeds. You just wish for anything you want."

"Well, I wish we were out of this cell," said Yang.

"No, no, wait," said Professor Bosh, but too late. There was a sudden whoosh, and they all found themselves on the other side of the cell door. Alas, they were still in the cellars of Mount Pipple-popple.

"You idiot," said the little flower. "You just wasted one."

"You have to be very specific," said the Professor. "Now we only have two seeds left. Let me handle this."

He took the two remaining seeds and looked at them closely. He selected the orange seed, put the yellow seed back in the honey jar, screwed the lid back on tightly, and then cleared his throat. "We have two wishes left, so we'll use one to get us to Bong and the other to stop the curse, agreed?"

"Sounds good to me," said Yang.

"Very well," said the Professor. "Firstly I *wish* that we were all on our way to Bong!"

No sooner had the words left his mouth than an orange cloud whipped round the corner and carried them off towards Bong.

"Well done," said Yin.

"You did great," added Yang. "We're out of there and on our way to Bong. Whatever is the matter?"

The Professor looked quite downcast. "I forgot to hold on

to the honey jar with the final seed," he confessed, "and we haven't stopped the curse."

Ten minutes later three puzzled henchmen were staring in disbelief at an empty but still locked cell.

"What do you mean they've gone?" said Flame.

"In two words: *im possible*," said Flicker.

"The cell is still locked," said Brimstone.

"He's really not going to believe us this time," said Flame nervously.

"Wait," said Brimstone, bending down to pick up the honey jar. "What's this?"

☄ Chapter
Twenty-seven

Pussycat and Pig were standing at the foot of the frozen rainbow. They had just found Owl's pocketknife.

"Owl climbed up the frozen rainbow," said the Pig. "See, there are the marks, then he must have slipped, 'cause he dropped his penknife, and then my guess is he slid into the Land of Water."

"How can you tell all that?"

"I had a cousin Sherlock Pig who was uncommonly good at deduction," said the Piggy-wig. "C'mon, lady, we got no time to lose. We'll take the rainbow."

"We'll never get up there," said Pussycat in alarm.

"Who said anything about *up*? We're going *down* the rainbow."

"*Down* the rainbow," said Pussycat. "But that's impossible."

"No, no," said the Pig. "Rainbows go up and down," and so saying, he cut a small hole in the frozen light with Owl's pocketknife and stuck his head in. Sure enough it was hollow with just enough room to squeeze inside. Pig lifted the cat up gently, said, "Keep your knees together," gave her a little shove, and off she went, sliding down inside the rainbow. The brightly glowing rainbow colors flashed as she slid past, and it reminded her of a ride at the fair. As she zoomed along inside the tube she could hear the Piggy-wig behind her.

"Isn't this great?" he yelled.

They were picking up speed and handling the ice curves with ease as they became accustomed to the slide. Faster and faster they went, and Pussycat was quite sorry when suddenly the frozen rainbow came to an abrupt end, and she was deposited in a pile of soft snow.

With a great flurry of flailing snow the Piggy-wig landed in an avalanche beside her. Together they looked around them. They were in a completely arctic world.

"What a pity," said Pig. "This place is so beautiful when it's water."

"Owly," yelled Pussycat hopefully as they commenced searching amongst the frigid figures. Her voice echoed mournfully around the icebergs. "Owly, where are you?"

"I do hope he ain't frozen," said the Pig.

Chapter Twenty-eight

"Soon be home, soon be home," sang the forest to the Bong Tree as it passed along its weary way. The sun had been obscured by clouds of swirling smoke for days, and the water holes where the tree would stop to soak its roots with a good long drink had all dried up. Now it was as cold and drear as winter. The poor tired tree was almost at the end of its tether as it stumbled into a clearing in the woods.

"Oh, dearie me, I am so exhausted," said the Bong Tree.

"Here, lie down and rest," said a kindly voice, which came from the mouth of a little old lady.

"I couldn't possibly, I'll be late. I'm due to flower today."

"I'll wake you up and make sure you're not late," said the voice. "You'll be much better for a nap." Fireflies flickered around its head.

"Watch out for those fireflies," said the Bong Tree. "Remember, I'm timber."

"Oh, sure you are. Wouldn't want anything happening to you, like *fire*, for instance."

The tree shuddered at the thought.

"See, I've made a special little bed for you, with lots of

straw, and some dry twigs and old leaves. That will make you very comfortable and keep you quite warm."

It looked just like a bonfire, but the thought of lying down for a while appealed to the tired tree.

"Perhaps I could use a short nap," said the tree, closing its eyes and lying down, as the old lady's hood fell away for a second to reveal the evil, glinting, mad eyes of the Fire Lord!

Chapter
Twenty-nine

Pussycat was beginning to despair of ever finding Owl in this arctic landscape.

"I'm feeling like frozen bacon at the moment, sweet thing. Can you hurry it up?" said Pig. "We've been searching for hours."

Pussycat was not about to give up because the Piggy-wig was cold, and she very determinedly pulled her fur around her and searched and searched until she finally found poor Owl frozen into a solid block.

"Oh, dear, he seems to be quite solid," said Pussycat sadly.

"Is this him?" asked Pig.

"Yes," said Pussycat in tears.

"He ain't much of a critter."

"That's only because he's frozen. You should see him when he's thawed. He can sing and he can fly . . ."

"Well, lady, it's *really* cold, and we found your frozen bird. Suppose we just get out of here."

"Good-bye, Owl. I really loved you. You were so brave. There will never be anyone else in my whole life to replace you."

"Lady, it's really cold, even for refrigerated pork. You want me to take a number and give you a call when he defrosts?"

"I must say good-bye properly. He was my true love, you know. Au revoir, Owly," and she gave him a farewell kiss on his frigid lips.

There came a loud cracking sound, as of ice breaking, the sound avalanches make when they burst off the side of snow-fields, and then a creaking sound like glaciers sliding down mountain slopes.

"What's that?" said the Pig anxiously.

"It's Owl," said Pussycat.

From somewhere deep within, her kiss had warmed his very being, and his little frozen heart began to beat faintly. Pig listened to his chest. "Lady, I think you're in luck. There's a pulse in this Popsicle," said the Pig excitedly.

Owl's glacial eyes began to crack like a frozen lake in springtime. The frost fell from his lids in tiny droplets like ice crystals melting on windowpanes, steam started out of his ears, and Owl began to stir from his deep, cold sleep. Pussycat's kiss had

melted his frozen heart with the warmth of her love. Pig was impressed.

"Lady, I seen some kisses, but that's the hottest yet."

But the biggest miracle of all was that everyone else began to thaw, warmed by the warmth of her love for Owl. She had broken the spell.

Chapter Thirty

The Bong Tree was snoring gently, blithely unaware of the danger it was in. The little old lady threw off her shawl to reveal the sulfurous figure of the Fire Lord.

"I shall control the world," he gloated. "I shall be the Emperor of Evolution. Nothing shall live except through my command," and with that he produced a large rope and bound the helpless tree. Now, even if it woke, the Bong Tree could not move.

High above his head, on a fast-moving orange cloud, Yin, Yang, and Professor Bosh shuddered as they looked down on this scene.

"He's got the Bong Tree prisoner," said Professor Bosh.

"Quickly," said Yin. "We must get help."

"Look," said Yang as their cloud flew underneath it, "the frozen rainbow is melting."

"You're right," said Professor Bosh excitedly. "Something must have broken the spell." They watched the frozen rainbow melt, becoming light and zooming off in all directions at a very great speed.

"Look, rainbow rain," said Professor Bosh. "That's a rare sight."

It was falling on the jam river and that, too, was beginning to thaw. The pea-green boat, frozen on the lip of the jamfalls, was slowly being freed from the ice and was once more in imminent danger of plunging to destruction on the rocks beneath. The small guitar sang anxiously for help, but alas they could not hear it.

"There they are!" yelled Yang excitedly as he spotted a soggy Owl embracing a very relieved Pussycat. They turned away from the jam river, leaving the pea-green boat teetering helplessly on the edge of the mighty jamfalls.

Chapter Thirty-one

"YOU have broken the spell and released us from our frozen state," said the Queen of the Water. "Whatever can we do to thank you?"

"You can help me with the riddle of the dinosaurs," said Owl.

"It's fairly obvious now," said the Queen.

Backwards through time
Till time stands still
And light is frozen cold,
Walk across the Land of Water
To the ring of gold.
Fur and feather hold together,
Will unite to change the weather.

"You crossed the Land of Water, and time was frozen cold. Now fur and feather hold together to change the weather. You, Owl, are feather, and Pussycat here is fur, and together you have melted the ice. See, the weather is indeed changing. The frozen rainbow is melting." They looked up in delight as rainbow rain covered them in different flavors. High above, colored light was arcing off into the sky.

"It's very lucky," said the Queen.

"But what about the ring?" said Owl and followed Pussycat's eyes to the end of Piggy-wig's nose. "Oh, I see. Mr. Pig—" But he was interrupted by the sudden descent of an orange cloud carrying two Pie-rats and Professor Bosh.

"Uncle," said Pussycat. "How wonderful to see you."

"Not so great to see you," said Owl to Yang. "You stole the Bong Tree seeds."

"It was an accident, honest," said Yin.

"We thought it was just honey," said Yang. "We'll make it up to you," he said as Owl advanced upon him.

"No time for that," said Professor Bosh. "The Fire Lord has trapped the Bong Tree."

There was a gasp of astonishment and fear from all the assembled throng.

"Right," said Owl decisively. "Hand over those seeds."

Pussycat looked at him in admiration. He seemed to have changed, to have become suddenly confident.

"Come on," said Owl firmly, "we must save the Bong Tree."

"Alas," said Professor Bosh, "we have no seeds left."

"Very well," said Owl, "we must do it by ourselves. Now, *this* is what I suggest. . . ."

Chapter
Thirty-two

Deep in the forest in a sheltered glade the Bong Tree stirred, struggling to wake up, but the bad dream would not go away. It couldn't seem to move its arms, and a sarcastic voice was gloating over it: "Slumber on, you useless piece of lumber. You're history, you're firewood."

It awoke to find itself pinioned by its branches with the ugly figure of the Fire Lord bending over it. "Finally woken up, have you? Well, you are at last my prisoner, in my power. It is time for me to rule the earth."

"You poor misguided power maniac," said the Bong Tree. "You think you can defeat evolution single-handedly?"

All the trees of the forest shook their branches at the Fire Lord and muttered loudly in Ancient Wood (a language spoken only by trees).

"They don't scare me, because they can't live without water, and I have frozen all the water!" said the Fire Lord, waving his arms dramatically above his head like a bad actor. He was showing off to impress the other trees, which was a big mistake, for suddenly there was a great slithering sound, and a huge white pile of snow slid directly onto his head. He was instantly buried in a mass of falling snow. He struggled out of the pile of snow with some irritation and looked around suspiciously at the trees.

"Who did that?"

Nobody answered. One of the trees giggled.

"Come on. I want to know who did that."

From the distance a tree blew a distinct raspberry. The Fire Lord was indignant.

"All right, I'll burn the lot of you. But first let me deal with the Bong Tree. Nobody shall stop me. Nobody."

"Wait. Stop!" said a voice.

The Fire Lord turned purple with rage. What had he just said? Who dared to stop him?

Into the clearing came his own three henchmen.

"How dare you!" he spluttered.

"Look, we have the Bong Tree seed," said Brimstone, holding up the honey jar. "Now you can find the Bong Tree."

"I have found the Bong Tree, idiots!" screamed the Fire Lord.

"Oh. Yes. Well, congratulations," said Brimstone.

"What are you going to do with it?" asked Flame.

"I shall watch it flower, steal its seed, maybe *dissect* it," he gloated.

"But you already have de seed," said Flicker, holding up the jar.

"That's right, so I do," said the Fire Lord. "I can simply take it back and grow it in my laboratory. I don't need this tree anymore. I can simply burn it."

"No..." whispered the trees of the forest.

"Well, that's just perfect. My triumph is complete. Say farewell to the legendary Bong Tree. No one shall interrupt me again," and with that he lit a match and leaned forward to set fire to the bonfire.

A small *Phattfacia* flower blew out the flame.

"Don't be ridiculous," said the Fire Lord, not even bothering to get angry, just striking another match. The flower blew it out again.

"What do you think you're doing?" said the Fire Lord testily. "Do you have any idea who I am?"

"Yes, you're the bully who set fire to my brother," said the *Phattfacia*. "I'm going to fix you good and proper." Of course, he was only playing for time.

"Right, I'm going to teach you a lesson," said the Fire Lord, standing up.

As he did so, a pie landed smack in his face. For a second he didn't know what hit him. He couldn't see anything. Flame, Flicker, and Brimstone seemed to be laughing at him.

"Who dared to do that?" said the Fire Lord, humiliated. Were his henchmen *really* laughing at him? Was he losing his power to terrify? "I'll show you," he said, wiping pie out of his eyes.

But he didn't get a chance to show anyone anything, for a huge volley of pies flew out of the woods, covering him from head to toe in a sticky mess.

"Charge!" yelled Yang, and out of the forest came the gang of Pie-rats, shouting and yelling to confuse their foe. At the sight of the rats screaming and doing kung-fu kicks, Flame, Flicker, and Brimstone turned tail and fled.

"You cowards!" yelled the Fire Lord. "Come back!" But they only ran faster. "Pyron, the flames!"

His dragon turned on the charging Pie-rats and breathed a blast of fire that sent them scurrying back for shelter.

"You think you can defeat me?" said the Fire Lord. "I am invincible." A snowball promptly hit him in the face.

"Good shot, Pussycat," said Owl, leaping into the air. He flew straight at the dazed Fire Lord, knocking him off his feet.

"Oh, so it's that ridiculous Owl, is it?" said the Fire Lord. "Pyron, torch him."

Owl was trapped on the ground, trying hard to flap his wings to escape, as the dragon turned on him and breathed in deeply. A moment later and Owl would have been singed to a cinder, but instead Pyron gave a loud scream. Pussycat had landed on his back and dug her claws in deeply.

The dragon broke into a run to escape the dreadful pain and disappeared out of the clearing at high speed. Pussycat leapt from his back into a tree as the maddened dragon ran headlong towards the jam river. The small guitar, marooned in the pea-green boat on the edge of the falls, could hear the creak of the timbers as the jam melted. In just a few seconds the boat would be totally free and plunge over the falls to destruction.

The guitar had almost given up hope when out of the woods at tremendous speed burst a maddened dragon, which slipped headlong on the melting jam, skidded out of control, banged into the pea-green boat, and sent it sliding across the ice to the safety of the far bank. The guitar leapt gratefully ashore while Pyron cannoned over the edge of the falls and was never seen again.

Pussycat ran up to Owl.

"Thank you, Pussycat," said Owl. "You saved my life."

"Only temporarily," said an extremely angry Fire Lord, for

he had lit the bonfire. The kindling burst into flames, and the Bong Tree struggled desperately to free itself.

"Look out, the bonfire's burning!" yelled Owl in alarm. He flew in, singeing his wings as the flames leapt up, but the fire was too strong for him and the bonfire blazed out of control.

Because of the intense heat Yin and Yang could not get close enough to pull the poor Bong Tree to safety. Through the smoke they could hear it groan, struggling hard to break its bonds. Even the Pig could not get near the blaze. The Fire Lord gave a terrible yell of triumph, but his triumph did not last long, for suddenly there was the Queen of the Water to the rescue with about a thousand water maidens.

"Hold on, Owl," she yelled as the water maidens bravely threw themselves onto the bonfire. Instantly they doused the flames, becoming great clouds of steam in the process. They had been ice maidens and now they were steam maidens, rising upwards in billows until they reached the cloud level, where they quickly became liquid again, falling as rain on the spreading blaze and putting it out.

Piggy-wig ran in to free the tree, cutting the ropes with Owl's pocketknife. Yin and Yang followed, and together they pulled the Bong Tree to safety.

"Hooray, the Bong Tree is free!" yelled the Pig, and they all began to cheer.

"NOT SO FAST!" Above the commotion the mad, calm voice of the Fire Lord commanded their attention.

"You have no chance," said Owl. "You might as well surrender."

"You forget I have the final seed!" said the Fire Lord, and he held it aloft in triumph.

"Don't eat it, whatever you do," warned the Bong Tree.

"You can't fool me like that. You think I was born yesterday? I am the mighty Fire Lord, and I shall—"

"No, really, you mustn't eat it," said Pussycat.

"Too late," said the Fire Lord. "Professor Bosh already told me I must eat the seed. So long, suckers," and he popped the final yellow seed into his mouth. At which he began to look distinctly sick. He seemed to be frozen and yet moving. His eyes flickered back and forth inside his head, and he was rooted to the spot.

"What's happened?" said Professor Bosh.

"He has become frozen in time," said the Bong Tree. "He cannot move either forwards or backwards. He is condemned to relive the same moment of his defeat over and over again. It is a very sad fate."

Not so sad that they couldn't all laugh at it, however.

"Serves him right," said the *Phattfacia,* and they all burst into a happy, optimistic whistling song, which is what *Phattfacias* like to do most of the time.

There was a great hallooing and yelling in triumph, and Owl embraced Pussycat and hugged Yin and Yang, all of whom were beside themselves with joy. The Queen of the Water was filled with pride at the bravery of her girls, and the Piggy-wig was dancing an extraordinary jig in celebration.

Owl turned to the beautiful cat with tears in his eyes. "Dear Pussycat, you have saved my life. Will you do me the honor of becoming my—" He became suddenly bashful.

"Your what?" said Pussycat helpfully.

"That is to say, I have no reasonable right to ask you, but life will not be worth living unless you are my—"

"Yes?" said Pussycat encouragingly.

The water maidens leaned in closer and nudged each other.

"Oh, Pussycat," said Owl, "will you marry me?"

"Of course I will, Owly," said Pussycat, "but what shall we do for a ring?"

The Pig cleared his throat and appeared to go cross-eyed, although he was in fact staring helpfully at the ring at the end of his nose. Pussycat followed his eyes.

"Mr. Pig, will you sell for one shilling your ring?" she asked politely.

"Sure I will," said the Pig. "I been thinkin' of retiring. I'm gonna get a little cabin up near the Jam Pits and just wallow around all day."

Everybody cheered and shook Owl's hand, and the Piggywig pulled the ring off his nose, and it made a perfect little wedding ring for Pussycat.

"Come on," said Owl, "let's get married!" And in no time at all the whole party found themselves marching up the hill to where the Turkey lived.

Chapter Thirty-three and a third

In a clearing at the top of a pleasantly wooded hill stood a tiny plasterboard chapel. An ancient white-wigged frog with an elaborate candelabra on its piano began to play the "Wedding April." (They never used the "Wedding March" there, because March was too cold for a wedding.) Pussycat was a glorious sight, and after a short ceremony full of nonsense (they were, after all, in Bong), the happy couple were married.

"I now pronounce you husband and teaspoon," said the Turkey in fluent Nonsense, and the crowd applauded. "You may now kiss the bride," he added, winking at Owl, who happily complied.

"Look!" gasped the crowd. "The Bong Tree is flowering."

The Bong Tree put on the most spectacular finale by bursting into flower. It blossomed into the most extraordinary display, throwing out colored lights in every direction to the great delight of the crowd.

Then everyone sat down to dine on mince and slices of quince, which they ate with a runcible spoon. Pussycat looked at Owl so happily, and he smiled at her contentedly. They had

saved the Bong Tree, their adventure was at an end, but their life together was only just beginning.

　　She rose into his arms while everyone clapped as the bride and groom began their wedding dance. The small guitar, seated on the deck of the pea-green boat, played the most romantic song, and soon everyone was dancing: the Piggy-wig, the Pie-rats, Yin and Yang, the water maidens in the waves, and even

Professor Bosh was waltzing with the Queen of the Water.

"Oh, Owly, I'm so happy," said Pussycat.

"Pussycat," said Owl, "you are the best of the best."

And hand in hand, on the edge of the sand, they danced by the light of the moon.

For Perry Ann Turnbull Callahan—
that you may know the lightness
of your mother's laughter.

    W. W.

The Owl and the Pussycat

The Owl and the Pussycat went to sea
    In a beautiful pea-green boat,
They took some honey, and plenty of money,
    Wrapped up in a five-pound note.
The Owl looked up to the stars above,
    And sang to a small guitar,
"O lovely Pussy! O Pussy, my love,
    What a beautiful Pussy you are,
        You are,
        You are,
What a beautiful Pussy you are!"

Pussy said to the Owl, "You elegant fowl!"
    How charmingly sweet you sing!
O let us be married! Too long we have tarried,
    But what shall we do for a ring?"
They sailed away for a year and a day,
    To the land where the Bong Tree grows,
And there in a wood a Piggy-wig stood
    With a ring at the end of his nose,
        His nose,
        His nose,
With a ring at the end of his nose.

"Dear Pig, are you willing to sell for one shilling
    Your ring?" Said the Piggy, "I will,"
So they took it away, and were married next day
    By the Turkey who lives on the hill.
They dined on mince, and slices of quince,
    Which they ate with a runcible spoon;
And hand in hand, on the edge of the sand,
    They danced by the light of the moon,
        The moon,
        The moon,
They danced by the light of the moon.

—EDWARD LEAR